N.M. Lance

This is truly the land of the Navajo. Monument Valley was "discovered" by the white man over 55 years ago. Here you will relive the events as our culture found the Navajo's culture. As much as this is a story of the Valley and the Navajo, it is a story of the pioneers: Harry and Mike Goulding, as well as the photographer Josef Muench.

*M*onument Valley is a land of everlasting wealth. The Navajo, the formations, the very color of the earth — all show you a warmth that enriches and excites the emotions.

Monument Valley, located on the border of northeastern Arizona and southeastern Utah, is a Navajo Tribal Park that preserves scenic values and the Navajo way of life.

Front cover: Totem pole and the Yeibichai. This 9x12 cm Kodachrome, taken in 1937, is the very first color photograph ever taken by Josef Muench. Inside front cover: John Cly. Page 1: Navajo child with her lamb. Pages 2/3: The Dunes area. Pages 4/5: The Mittens and Merrick Butte; also taken in 1937, this view is the second color photograph ever taken by Josef Muench.

Edited by Mary L. Van Camp.
Book design by K. C. DenDooven.

Third Printing, 1993.
MONUMENT VALLEY: THE STORY BEHIND THE SCENERY
© 1992, KC PUBLICATIONS, INC.

LC 92-70430 ISBN 0-88714-062-9.

MONUMENT VALLEY
THE STORY BEHIND THE SCENERY®

Photography by Josef Muench.

Josef came to Monument Valley in 1936, took his first photographs, and has been back 354 times. His sensitivity for the Navajo and love of the land is reflected throughout the book.

Text by K. C. DenDooven.

K. C. came to the Valley in 1962 when he first entered the publishing world. Here he met Harry Goulding who gave him an insight into the magnificence and grandeur of the great Southwest.

This is Monument Valley, a land of profound beauty. Much of the Southwest occupied today by Indian tribes are places the white man didn't want, land he felt to be worthless. Today we all take pleasure in visiting this same land, photographing its rich colors, marveling at its unspoiled beauty. The Navajo and unknown tribes before live with the land. They use it as a source of life.

The Valley has monuments, lots of them. Dramatic sandstone spires, arches, shapes and forms. One could say these magnificent formations have arisen from a sea of sand. Others, more geologically correct, can see the vertical edifices as leftovers after the forces of erosion descended on a sandstone plateau.

This is a land to behold. A land to use with our eyes. It will instill great emotional values. It is a gift from the Creator.

The shape and shadows of Moccasin Arch fulfill its name to all who visit it. Navajos love to be the colorful accents to their proud land.

View from Hunt's Mesa.

The Valley

Everything in life is a matter of perspective. Here we see dramatic sandstone monuments. To the Navajo the Valley is home. To the first-time visitor it is one of the most awesome spectacles of nature he has ever seen. To those of us who have been here many times it is a great place to revisit again and again, a place of beauty and memories — yet a place where we know there is always something more to see and enjoy.

Monument Valley is a land of people, of formations, of mystery and mood. In the winter it can snow enough to literally stop you in your tracks. In the summer it can be very unforgiving to those who don't bring enough water.

The arches and bridges (Harry called them "holes") are just present-day stages in a geologic evolution that started millions of years ago and will continue on forever.

THE DESERT

At a quick glance this land looks like a dry, dusty, barren desert. Desert it is — but with life all around you. The Navajo live here in a world that is theirs. They raise families and tend sheep. There is water; trees and flowers do grow; children have fun, go to school, work, play. The desert floor teems with life — you just have to look for it.

Back in 1938, Hollywood was astounded to find out that there *was* a real West, complete with real, live Indians. They could leave their make-believe back lots and produce movies in the *real* West. "Stagecoach" was shot here. A young actor by the name of John

"Nowhere in the world can one find a similar effect of nature's work. Words alone, the thousand-foot pyramid and castles, the slender tower, bridges and arches — cannot begin to describe the sandstone formations that dominate Monument Valley."

Josef Muench.

Wayne would be discovered. Director John Ford would find his "point." Western towns would appear (and disappear) — but more of that later.

Visiting Monument Valley is a great experience for there is much to be seen. As you go over the next hill or around the next bend a unique world unfolds in front of you. Besides an extraordinary geologic history there is a great human history that goes well back in time, even before the Navajo. We will not understand everything we see here in just one tour or one experience. Those who can return again and again do so because it is a land of intrigue.

The present-day scene is a little different than it was in the late '30s. The Navajo have traded in their wood-spoked wagons for pickup trucks. The road to Monument Valley is now paved. Now there are air-conditioned motels with all the modern trappings.

Navajo Tribal Park

This is a Navajo Tribal Park. The tribe maintains a visitor center, monitors tours into the Valley, and patrols the area so it will be enjoyable for those here today and preserved for those who will come next year and in future decades.

But the mood of the people and the look of the proud rugged land is always here. You get a sense of adventure even as you drive down the highway adjacent to Monument Valley. Actually, the Arizona-Utah state line runs just about through the middle. Who cares? Nature didn't. The Navajo doesn't. Monument Valley is here, to be shared and viewed by all.

Navajo horsemen add the feeling of presence to the dramatic North Window.

A Valley Full of Arches

▲ **F**ull Moon Arch is typical of the open formations in Monument Valley. It is a present-day statement in an involved geologic process. Nature finds a weak spot in the thin sandstone cliff. Be it a crack or a small hole in the vertical face, the elements drive against the rock to open the sandstone to daylight and sky. Winter rain and snow followed by freezing and thawing work the cracks till larger chunks fall out. But always it's the wind and blowing sand that rounds off the edges. Will it last? No, it's just a phase. When the top collapses we'll see a U-shaped opening. In time the entire wall will come down as the geologic process happens and moves on.

Called Swinnerton ▶
Bridge, this high-up formation was named after the artist/ cartoonist Jimmy Swinnerton. Names applied to virtually all the formations in Monument Valley are the white man's view of things. Sure the Navajo have names for these places, but — in Navajo!

◀ **H**idden Bridge shows evidence of the water flowing over and through the opening. To those who wonder, a bridge is a rock span that was undercut by a flow of water. An arch is a span created by weathering, like Full Moon Arch on the opposite page.

11

Sheep - Wool - The Way of Life

The Navajo's life in Monument Valley revolves around sheep more than any other single entity. The two main trading commodities of the Navajo are wool and woven rugs. Both are products regenerated annually from their flocks of sheep. The land simply will not support enough grass for great numbers of sheep to be raised and sold like cattle.

In years past people brought wool to Goulding's Trading Post to buy commodities. Today they are more apt to take the wool to a larger city in pickups. While it is a time-consuming process, some of the wool is woven into beautiful Navajo rugs, especially during the long winter months. Just the presence of the sheep themselves is of economic value. They are photographed daily being driven down sand dunes in areas seen by visitors (pages 2/3). Sheep and goats are also a source of food.

▲ **Springtime means shearing time. It's always a family** affair and the sheep are treated carefully, almost like pets, for their wool will be needed again and again. It may seem hard for a first-time visitor to believe, but this is the very beginning of a beautiful and valuable Navajo rug.

...and Flowers Too

◀ **If you ever wondered** about the "purple sage" in western tales, well, this is it. The red sands provide an even more dramatic background. Like all the plants, flowers, and trees in the Valley they grow when and where there is adequate moisture. The root system draws up what it needs. If there's not enough rainfall this year the plant goes dormant. It doesn't die. Sudden rain will make the desert bloom again in a myriad of shapes and colors.

*◄ **F**ew large trees grow in Monument Valley. There just isn't enough water to support many. This silhouetted cottonwood is an exception. Navajos prefer not to camp or stay close to a tree. They feel their presence disrupts the root system. Also, maybe they know more about lightning strikes than we do!*

***S**nakewood ▶ gets its name for good reason. The Navajo know to give it proper respect since the dense bush makes an ideal spot for a rattlesnake to get away from the intense sun.*

*◄ **C**liffrose supplies more than just a pretty subject to photograph. The shrub beneath the blossoms is called babybrush by the Navajo since they use its shredded bark as a soft mattress in their babies' cradleboards. In back, one of the Mittens dominates the skyline with its bold presence.*

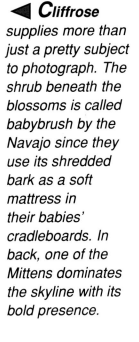

*◄ **C**ontrast. The brilliant red signifies this as a low spot where moisture and fine silt collect. The rocks in the Valley really are this red. A small rabbitbrush accents the background.*

Mystery Valley — Land of Intrigue

▲ **What dramatic views you can get in Monument Valley by combining unique formations with** the proper camera angle. A double arch can be a sinister face. Who has more fun, nature or the photographer?

◄ **Honeymoon Arch.** Another name created by our imagination. There is a small ruin under the far side of the archway which will accommodate just two people. If the white man had built it he probably would have put it out in front and in the center. The Anasazi knew better. He located the dwelling off to the side so it wouldn't be seen by an enemy or washed away by the next flash flood.

▲ **In Mystery Valley,**
Natural Arch presents a
feeling of balance and
symmetry. Harry, who
found this formation
decades ago, provides
human scale to show off
the size of the arch.

Caves provide not only ▶
shelter from the elements, but
they can be adapted into homes,
granaries, and at times be set up
for religious purposes. Again,
this site is in Mystery Valley.

▲ *Flash flood — an awesome sight in the Southwest. Rain clouds off in the distance can produce a driving river down into an area where the sun still shines brightly.*

The Forces of Nature that Created the Land

The Three ▶
Sisters refer to three nuns not three siblings. Here it's easy to see the two mature nuns leading the thin young initiate between them. Isn't creative imagination wonderful!

Sometimes called ▶
El Capitan, this 1,400-foot-high volcanic plug is a remnant of the intense volcanic action that took place in the Southwest. What we see here is the hard center core of a volcano after the softer outer rocks have been eroded away. Wind and water are the forces that have carved everything we see in the Valley.
The Navajo call this the Agathla (A-gath-la) which means "The place of the scraping of the hides." Here, periodically, the sheep are shorn of their wool, and the people of the Valley enjoy a pow-wow (a social gathering and celebration).

*"**H**appy" Cly grooms the hair of her husband, Willie Cly.*

The Navajo

The Navajo is one of the most interesting tribes to observe and learn about. They are by far the largest Indian tribe in North America. More than 180,000 live on their Reservation which is about the size of West Virginia. Window Rock, the capital, is the closest to what you'd call a city. Kayenta, just south of Monument Valley, is more typical of the towns within their land. They call their Reservation The Navajo Nation, and in many ways they do operate like a small independent country surrounded by a very large country.

Navajos are nomads and adapters. They live off the land. They live by their rules and at their own pace — both of which in many ways are distinctly different from the white man's. Sheep and wool are one of the main forms of industry throughout the entire Navajo land. Sheep wander — Navajos wander, and both live where the conditions are workable.

Their entire history shows a life style of adaptation. Their language is derived from the Athabascan-speaking tribes of northwest Canada. Much of their agriculture relates back to the Apache and Pueblo Indians. Yet they

"This atmosphere is not a figment of the imagination. Here is a blend of cultures from deep-rooted ways of the ancient ones to pickup trucks and self-winding watches. Colorfully dressed women match the beauty of the red sandstone in which they live. Monument Valley is their home."

Josef Muench.

do not build stone homes. Their hogan (hō-gän) is a well-engineered home for the desert, cool in the summer — warm in the winter.

When the Spaniards arrived with horses, it made sense to the Navajo so they adapted the horse, or more correctly the Navajo pony which is a lighter-weight, somewhat short-legged horse. The wood-spoked wagon was fine until the development of the pickup truck. Today a wagon's only use is for photographers, parades, and to show visitors what life was like in the "old days."

They believe in the Medicine Man. He still performs healing ceremonies, but they will also go to the Monument Valley Hospital. Many Navajos when sick play it safe — go to the hospital *and* see the Medicine Man.

NAVAJO RUGS

Navajo rugs are prized for their quality and beauty. The money the Indians get for selling a Navajo rug may well be used for buying a Pendleton blanket since it's warmer. Many of their arts and crafts (rugs, silver and turquoise, decorated baskets and pottery) came about because traders such as Harry Goulding pointed out that they could earn money by making quality arts and crafts.

Here in Monument Valley you see the Navajo as he lives today, but with reminders of the way of life as it has evolved over the last 50 years. Roads to get to the Valley are now paved. But roads in the Valley vary from graded gravel to four-wheel-drive (requiring Navajo guides), to just hiking trails.

Perhaps it could be said best that Monument Valley serves as their showplace. The Navajo's window into their unique world. They are proud of their land — and rightly so. It has a beauty and majesty all of its own. Here you are a visitor to the life-style of the Navajo.

A Navajo family ▶ in front of The Three Sisters. Hogans always face the east. This is both tradition and a practical use of the sunrise's warming rays. The sheep are normally out in the Valley. Horses are still very much in use. The photogenic rug loom is generally outside the hogan except in winter or bad weather.

▲ *R*ug weaving inside the hogan. The raw wool next to the mother is being cleaned and carded by the daughter. Both will work at dyeing wool and spinning it into usable yarn. The prep work to get wool ready for weaving is often longer than it takes to weave the rug. This pattern is more modern than the one seen on the opposite page or below.

◄ *T*he two-gray-hills rug is typical of those made in the eastern part of the Reservation. Most weavers produce a great variety of patterns depending on their mood or the requests placed by traders.
K.C. DEN DOOVEN

▲ **In summer a family will live and work in a covered shelter, usually close to their**
hogan. If the best area for their sheep is a bit too far away, they will establish a "summer
home" close to the flocks. Life on the Reservation is very much a family affair with all
members working together.

The difficulty the Navajo, in fact all Indian tribes, face is that money and jobs lie outside
in the white man's world. But their culture, roots, and families are still back on their own land.
So, they tend to go back and forth to try and balance their monetary needs with their
spiritual needs. It is a very real and very complex problem.

Overleaf: One of ▶
the many moods of
the Valley, from
Hunt's Mesa
(compare with page 8).

23

Dineh: The People

◀ **A Navajo woman, her** blouse bedecked with silver and beadwork of the '40s, stands in front of a partially completed storm-pattern rug. The coins are dimes which adapt well as decoration jewelry. Quarters and half-dollars were used, but usually not silver dollars (cost? weight?). The silver and turquoise they wore was their "bank." Where else could they keep their wealth? No banks here, and paper money did not seem real. Consider the "buying power" of a quality turquoise and silver necklace.

The cradleboard ▶ was a practical invention of the Indian people. A loop at the top provided a sun shield when the mother carried the child on her back. The board could be set down without disturbing a sleeping baby. Babybrush was used inside for padding — the original biodegradable solution to an age-old situation.

▲ **The look of age and wisdom. Taken** in the '40s, this photograph by Josef Muench illustrates much of the Navajo's outlook back then.

▲ **The velveteen blouse and satin skirt with silver and** turquoise were proper attire to be worn for photographers.

The lives of a ▶ young girl and her mother were busy and provided a lot of closeness as they worked and played together. The daughter helped card wool, learned to cook and sew, and watched after the sheep, unless there was an older brother to do this.

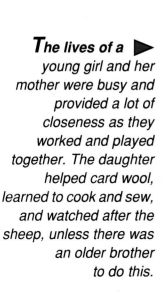

Anasazi Petroglyphs & Pictographs

▲ **A**n ancient pot unearthed by the shifting sand and photographed in 1963 exactly where it was found.

◀ **P**etroglyphs — why here? The same reason humans do things in specific places — for a specific reason. This was dry desert country even 10,000 years ago. Eking out a life was difficult — no time for meaningless doodles. This is rock writing. Inscriptions to convey information to be read and understood. We need to preserve this and learn more about its intended message.

Kay-tso, an old ▶ Medicine Man, shows a section of a large panel in the Valley. Rock writing stopped about the time of the coming of the white man. Indians back then were unsure who they could trust (they still are!). Today few of any of the tribes can read petroglyphs. The study of just what information was recorded is a present-day challenge.

◀ Pictographs, that is painted images, come close to being an art form. The hand symbols were used in many areas and could be an ancient way of saying "I was born here." These markings in Mystery Valley have stood centuries of time. Too bad our modern house paint and printing ink can't be as good!

There are not ▶ many large ruins in Monument Valley. These are just south of the Valley proper, toward Kayenta. The formations in Monument Valley did not produce too many large natural caves or overhangs. The techniques of construction are fairly common throughout the Southwest. Mesa Verde, Canyon de Chelly, Chaco, and the Navajo National Monument all have larger dwelling sites.

Sand Painting and a Healing Ceremony

Sand paintings were created as a part of a healing ceremony performed by the Medicine Man — usually an elder in the village or area. While he uses herbs and natural plants, the sand painting ceremony is more like a form of prayer. In a case like this photo sequence the man is healing the mind, cleansing the soul.

▲ **F**irst the ground must be ▶ prepared. Special fine sand is brought in to be spread on the smooth ground. The girl up on the hillside with her family watches the Medicine Man making his preparations. This girl was tending a flock of sheep when a rattlesnake crossed her path. It did not bite her, but she needs the ceremony to take away fear, take away any worries that the snake will return.

◀ **A**fter the various colored rocks are ground up (above) the design is made. Here we see the Yei figures. A Yei is a masked representative of a supernatural being which possesses great power. Over 600 different designs are used in sand paintings, depending on the need.

▲ *The girl now sits in the middle of the sand painting. This is her ceremony. The Medicine Man will do chants, and communicate to the Yeibichai figures in Navajo mythology. He has a medicine bundle from which he has drawn elements to help the healing process. The girl, and her family, has total faith in this man to remove the mental and emotional cloud so that she can go forward and not worry about any evil happening from the past event. Seldom are outsiders allowed to photograph an actual healing ceremony. Josef Muench's long years of work with the Navajo, especially at Monument Valley, gave him the opportunity to take these pictures in 1960. Once completed the painting will be destroyed, and the sand collected to be taken back to where it was originally obtained.*

Harry and Mike in 1945.

"Let me call you 'Mike'." — Harry Goulding was moving into this Arizona/Utah country to establish a new life with his new bride. Her given name was just too much for him to remember. He had sheep to take care of, household effects to move across the desert. They were moving into a land where nobody spoke English. So, Mike it was — now he could concentrate on his other problems.

Born in Durango, Colorado, in 1897, he moved from a ranch near Aztec, New Mexico, to Monument Valley in 1923. A Model-T made the journey across the sandy desert. Roads then, at best, were little more than trails. A sheepherder by trade, Harry lived off the land, just like the Navajo. He established the trading post and began to set down his roots.

Not only did Harry and Mike understand and befriend the Navajo through a half-century of business, but they really are the people who brought Monument Valley to the world. Perhaps it would be better to say they brought the world to Monument Valley.

Subsequent to their arrival in the Valley, the stock market crash of '29 wiped out nearly any chance for business. The Valley was there, the Navajo lived off the land, but Harry needed to find a monetary source. The solution presented itself in the late '30s when Harry learned that Hollywood was going to make a western movie to be called "Stagecoach." He decided he'd be a one-person ambassador for the Valley.

"Stagecoach" Arrives

And he did it! After "Stagecoach," "My Darling Clementine," "She Wore a Yellow Ribbon," "Fort Apache," "The Searchers," and many more were shot on location in the

> *"Like the fine rugs that the Navajo women weave, so too are the finest of people associated with Monument Valley — Harry and Mike (Leona) Goulding. They settled here as traders in 1923 and put names to many of the monuments in this, the heart of Navajoland."*
>
> **Josef Muench.**

Valley. Movie companies hired Navajos and spent a lot of money. This was only the beginning.

Harry's work directly and indirectly led to many friendships such as with Josef Muench whose photos in "Arizona Highways" magazine publicized the Valley. Lots of magazine articles both in this country and throughout the world started to tell about this extraordinary land.

If you never saw Monument Valley, but only photos of it, you'd wonder if this place was for real. Even after Hollywood made the decision in 1938 based on Josef's photos, they still chartered a plane to see for themselves that this Valley and its monuments really existed.

Those who knew Harry and Mike knew their love and respect for the Navajo was very profound. Not only did they want to bring people to see the Valley and to help the local Indians become employed, they also worried about the Navajo's health.

Harry knew the Medicine Men and respected their value. Harry also knew a modern hospital and doctors were needed. In the '60s he arranged for the Seventh-Day Adventists to build and establish a hospital just around the bend from his trading post. He leased them the land for $1 per year on a 99-year lease, and then gave much personal financial support.

People don't start life with a game plan or purpose — it evolves, it happens. Harry had a calling to live among and help the Navajo people. Mike shared it with him each and every day. Josef Muench had a calling to be a photographer. Although he has taken many dramatic photographs all over the world, perhaps his greatest work was a small, 8x10 black and white album done back in 1938.

Goulding's Trading ▶
Post was designed and built by Harry and Mike in 1928. The Navajos who helped them had never before seen a two-story stone building. Today the post is a recognized national landmark as well as a functioning museum in the same trading-post style that served the Navajo for over 60 years.

ENTRANCE

GOULDING
GOULDINGS MUSEUM

▲ *Two Navajo women and their ponies stand on Ford's Point. This is the spot where* director John Ford liked to set his camera to capture a Navajo on horseback or the "hero" out on the point to the right. Visitors often mistake the actor's place for "the" Ford's Point.

Tombstone, ▶
Arizona, as it was rebuilt in
Monument Valley, Arizona
— for the movie "My
Darling Clementine." Just
for the record, all the
magnificent background is
in Utah. Sets like this are
completely removed after a
movie is shot. The desert
lives on.

The Movies Come to Monument Valley

"Stagecoach": 1938

Harry knew something had to be done. There was no money, no income, no future. The scenery was fabulous but nobody ever saw it. He told Josef Muench he planned to go to Hollywood to convince them to use the Valley to make movies.

Harry was going to use simple snapshots that people had sent him — box camera stuff. Josef knew Harry would never succeed with those photos. He said he'd make up a special album of black and white pictures (color film was just invented, Hollywood wasn't using it yet). So off Harry and Mike went — with canned goods from the shelves of their trading post for food enroute.

When the receptionist at United Artists gave Harry a brush-off he told her that was OK, he'd brought a bedroll and would just roll it out in the lobby! Harry always was a very patient man. To get rid of him, a location manager came to the lobby. One look at the photos and off he went with the pictures. A bit later the photographs were laid out in front of John Ford and production chief Walter Wanger, with Harry describing the Valley.

Hollywood was in its flamboyant era. Top men made decisions on the spot. Committees hadn't been invented yet! Within a few hours the die was cast. Monument Valley *was* the place.

Parts of Harry's story tell a lot about him and the era. Wanger said that he'd contact Babbitts in Flagstaff to arrange for needed supplies to be shipped to the Valley. (By the way, at that time the paved road stopped at Tuba City.) Ford and Wanger said that Harry would also need money for things to have on hand. So they gave him a check which he just folded and put in his pocket.

On their way back to the Valley, in Williams, Arizona, Harry and Mike ran low on gas — not enough to make it to Flagstaff, 33 miles east. "No problem," said Harry, "they gave me a check." And he pulled into a local gas station. Remember this was in 1938, the depression era. The check made out to Harry was for *Five Thousand Dollars!* The station man said it was the best laugh he had had in ages, gave Harry two gallons and sent him on his way.

When Harry and Mike did arrive in Flagstaff they saw a long run of stake trucks lined up on both sides of the street in front of Babbitt Brothers General Store. Harry met Ed Babbitt out in front and asked, "What's going on?" "Harry, you tell me what's going on—Hollywood is on the phone every half-hour adding to the list of items to be shipped to the Valley."

And thus the Valley was discovered for all to see, in person or in movie houses worldwide.

▲ *Harry, back in the '40s, dealing with a Navajo woman. Note her Pendleton blanket.*
Sometimes things were bought with actual cash money, but more often barter or credit was the form of transfer. Turquoise and silver jewelry could be pawned, to be paid off when the sheared wool was brought in or Navajo rugs were delivered to the trading post. Harry virtually never sold a pawned item.

Maurice Knee starts ▷
to fill an order at the counter. A trading post was far more than just a country store. It was where people met, exchanged local news, learned what else was happening in the world (if they cared!). Problems were solved, and disagreements settled. A good trader was a respected judge and jury in these remote areas.

Family

In the living room ▷ at the trading post the family gathers. Left to right: Mike; Harry; Maurice (Mike's brother); Mrs. Knee (mother of Maurice and Mike); and Harry's Aunt Molly. It took unique people to live and operate back in the '40s–'50s. Morris Knee's brother Lurt Knee and his wife operated the lodge at the south end of Capitol Reef. Harry was a distant cousin to Art Greene who started the operations at Wahweap, before there was a Lake Powell. (Note: The photo over the fireplace is one of Josef Muench's.)

▼ **Harry and Mike had to be morning people. Their home faced the east, like a hogan. Sunrises** signaled the beginning of a brand new day. Their life had to be a great adventure. They did what they wanted to do, when it needed to be done. They answered only to the supreme being of life and the orderly balance of nature. This is the scene they enjoyed each morning, and ultimately brought the world to Monument Valley so it could be shared.

Josef Muench working with one of his favorite subjects.

Josef G. Muench — a man who at age 23, in 1927, actually hit Adolph Hitler with a tomato he threw, and lived to tell the story — is not just the photographer of this book; he is almost as much a part of the Monument Valley story as Harry and Mike Goulding.

Each of us is a part of the great scene. Harry and his Navajo friends lived the Valley. But until Josef's photos appeared in "Arizona Highways" and his work was spread out in Walter Wanger's Hollywood office — the Valley was unknown, unseen, and unvisited.

Like most intriguing stories, the beginning is far away. Josef was born February 8, 1904, in Schweinfurt, Germany. When he was 12 his mother gave him his first camera, a simple box style she had received from her employer at Christmas.

Taking photos of friends and selling them the pictures for pennies allowed Josef to buy his next camera for ten marks (about $10.00 then). He was on his way to his destiny.

JOSEF MOVES TO AMERICA

At the Hitler incident there had been S.S. officers sitting on both sides. Hitler was just an emerging radical then, but Josef knew when he and his followers came to power they would remember his defiance. He would be a marked man. So, Josef left his homeland and came to the United States in 1928, and got a job with the Ford Motor Company.

The urge to see the entire United States was great. As soon as he could afford a Model-A roadster ($535, cash) and save up $300 for travelling money, Josef headed west.

Reaching Santa Barbara, California, on

"Having seen that Desertscape now hundreds of times, it is no longer possible to remember what it looked like the first time. I can no longer capture a state of mind in which Monument Valley was not a part of my mental and emotional equipment."

Josef Muench.

November 15, 1930, he decided that this would be his new home. The swaying palms and breaking surf were just too appealing for Josef to look elsewhere.

Taking photographs was his love, his life, his future. But, in 1930, with a 25-percent unemployment figure, his more pragmatic side told Josef to take a job as a gardener at St. Francis Hospital. Today his home, the same one he bought in '34, is a good display of his gardening skills.

His first commercial sale was an 8x10 black and white photo of a bus for a cover on "Trailways Magazine." $5.00 in 1931. He was back on the trail to his destiny.

"Arizona Highways," the Valley, and Kodachrome

Josef met Raymond Carlson, the driving force who turned "Arizona Highways" from a state road construction magazine into today's very well known scenic publication. Josef left Raymond fifty 8x10 black and whites to review in '36. Eventually the magazine published every one of those photographs.

After his first trip to Monument Valley in 1935, he returned with his wife, Joyce, in '37. Joyce was a writer, so the two teamed up on a story about the Valley which appeared in "Arizona Highways" in '39.

Eastman Kodak came out with Kodachrome in 1937. In that year Josef shot his first color photograph. Where else?! (It is this book's cover photo.) In working on this Monument Valley book Josef made his 354th trip into the Valley, at age 87. His love and respect for the Navajo, Harry Goulding, and the Valley have never diminished.

▼ *In the '40s the roads into the Valley were a couple of ruts in a sandy trail. The wildflowers blossomed, the Navajo lived their way of life, and Monument Valley was about to be rediscovered.*

The Navajos in Their Valley

◀ **Josef enjoys his** relationship with the Navajo. Who else could get them to bring out their own simple cameras to pose for a photo. Now if only we could see what they were taking a picture of — tourists or scenery?

Lunch time in ▶ the Valley. The Navajo has very strong family ties. The man on the left is not a relative, but since he had no family he's been "adopted" by the others. This is the way of the Indians, they recognize one's need for being part of a family.

▲ **M**onument Valley is a photographer's (or movie maker's) dream come true. The spires, the clouds, the clean air, the open spaces, the colorful Navajos, the ponies, the sheep, the sand dunes — all of these are elements that individually make for good picture material. Here they can be combined into one single photograph!

People who return time after time feel cheated if the sky is cloudless. The patterns created on the Valley floor, the monuments that dance in and out of the shadows are such that from a single spot you can shoot many different pictures in a matter of minutes.

The North Window is a favorite of all photographers, from those with a simple camera to movie directors and ad-agency executives. The Navajo are very used to being photographed. Some are sort of pros who feel they should be paid to have their picture taken. And why not? — They are being used as models. Even their horses know how to pose. Kodak today still uses the Valley as a subject to demonstrate the quality of its film. They know that Monument Valley is one of the most photographed sites anywhere in the world. And rightly so.

Working with Light - Snow - People - A Love of the Land

Harry and ▲ one of his Navajo friends talk about "their" Valley. A natural setting in this dramatic country.

◄ **There are some** unique areas in the Valley that require searching out. Rooster Rock in front of the thousand-foot-high Meridian Butte is just one of these special places.

Yes, it does snow in  the Valley. Occasionally up to three or four feet. A light blanket of the white stuff is great to accent the form and color of this red-rock country.

In the '40s this ▶ was the view from the trading post's front door. The stone building was reserved for John Ford when he was there either to shoot a movie or just relax and enjoy the Valley.

▲ *The he Valley never changes and yet it's always different! This scene taken in 1990 is similar to the 1937 photo on the cover. The 808-foot-high totem pole has been scaled and even used in auto commercials. A convertible was slung onto the top by a helicopter! Today the Navajo shy away from such usage of their monument. The formation in behind is called the Yeibichai after dancers of their mythology.*

Everybody is swept up by the charm of Monument Valley although for vastly different reasons. Beauty is in the eyes of the beholder. Certainly this Valley is a perfect example of that philosophy.

SUGGESTED READING

MARTINEAU, LA VAN. *The Rocks Begin to Speak*. Las Vegas, Nevada: KC Publications, Inc., 1973.

MOON, DR. SAMUEL. *Tall Sheep*. Norman, Oklahoma: University of Oklahoma Press, 1992.

REED, ALLEN C. *Grand Circle Adventure*. Las Vegas, Nevada: KC Publications, Inc., 1983.

There is so much to see in the Valley. Yet, it 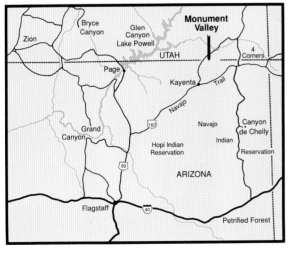 *is the dramatic symbols that catch the eye and are most remembered by the viewers, and their cameras! The "Totem Pole," the Navajos and their sheep coming down the dunes, and here we have the "Mittens." Framed by well-placed juniper, these "hands-of-time" welcome you near the entrance to Monument Valley — or, are they saying goodbye as you leave? Perhaps it may be best said that they stand as friendly signs from the Navajo people, asking you to return again and again.*

◀ Monument Valley is at 5,200-foot elevation, north of *Kayenta, Arizona, along the Navajo Trail. The Valley is along the Arizona-Utah border. Roads are open all year long, but there is snow during the winter.*

Monument Valley is a place to let your thoughts run wild. You'll see shapes and forms in this dramatic display of nature. One can "see" the adventures and stories unfold. Across the sandy Valley you can feel the hand of God building his creation. It's hard to imagine that this once was just a 1,000-foot layer of solid sandstone.

A sculptor was once asked how he carved a horse out of a block of granite. "Simple," he said, "just take away everything that doesn't look like a horse." So God started with one hundred square miles of sandstone and just took away everything that didn't look like Monument Valley! And now it's ours — to appreciate and enjoy. An untouched creation of nature that touches us all.

Full moon and the "King on his Throne," "The Stagecoach," "Bear and the Rabbit," with the "Big Indian" on the right. What a world for a vivid imagination.

47

▲ *The Valley in all its splendor. Eroded layers of rich red earth, the monuments in their majesty.*
Enough plant life to add touches of green and provide habitat for its little creatures. To top it off a selection of fluffy clouds. As Josef Muench once commented, "I feel lonely when I don't have any clouds."

Inside back cover: The ▶
Mittens reach for the sky
at sunrise.

Back cover: The Navajo, ▶
protector of the Valley. The Valley,
home of the Navajo.

Books on Indian Culture and the Southwest: Southwestern Indian Arts and Crafts, Southwestern Indian Ceremonials, Southwestern Indian Tribes, Canyon de Chelly, Glen Canyon-Lake Powell, Grand Circle Adventure, The Rocks Begin to Speak.

Published by KC Publications • The Story Behind the Scenery
Box 94558 • Las Vegas, NV 89193-4558

Created, Designed and Published in the U.S.A.
Printed by Dong-A Printing and Publishing, Seoul, Korea
Color Separations by Kedia/Kwangyangsa Co., Ltd.